EVERYONE IS A DESIGNER IN THE AGE OF SOCIAL MEDIA
Concept and Design: Mieke Gerritzen
Editors: Geert Lovink and Mieke Gerritzen
Production by All Media Foundation, Amsterdam
Published by BIS Publishers
First Edition 2010
ISBN 978-90-6369-227-8

HOME NEWS ABOUT PROJECTS WHO CONTACT

EVENTS SETTINGS TIMETABLE LOG OUT BLOGROL

ADVERTISE CONTRIBUTE TOPICS PEOPLE ACTIVITIE

ANSWERS FOR STUDENTS HOW WE DO IT LOCATION

OFFERINGS COMPANY PARTNERS REACH US WHAT MA

PORTFOLIO STATISTICS FREE TOOLS JOBS PUB

GET LISTED LOGIN REVIEWS RESEARCH IN DEVE

STATEMENT MORE GET ART BECOME A FRIEND TO

ADD ME TO YOUR NETWORK RECENT COMMENTS CREATIVE COM

REMEMBER ME FORGOT YOUR PASSWORD? BOOKSHELF

FRIENDS BROWSE LOGOUT DO YOU WANT MORE?

AMATEURS DIY WE THINK OUTSOURCE FEEL GOOD

DOWNLOAD PUT TYPE COLLECT EXHIBITIONS

LATEST HEADLINES GETTING STARTED MOST VISITED

MEDIA NEW HISTORY OUR WORLD DISCOURS

MAPS TRANSLATION HANDBOOK PRINT FEED SU

CONTRIBUTE SCHEDULE SPEAKERS HOW-TOS SECTI

SUBSCRIBE NOW GROUPS LINKS IMPRINT FOLLO

CALENDAR PRINT THIS PAGE UPDATE YOUR BAG STORE

SEARCH | FRIENDS | **ABOUT YOUR TRIP** | PROFILE | INBOX

FOLLOW | HOW YOU CAN HELP | RECENT POSTS | LAB

ORGANISATION | FRIENDS | NEW WORK | OLDER WORK

ANY | INFO | CLIENT LIST | OFFICES/CONTACT | IDEAS

S TO YOU? | WHAT'S NEW? | ARCHIVE | PREVIEW | MYSPACE

IONS | POPULAR | SERVICES | DIRECTORY | BE A FAN

MENT | IN PRODUCTION | HOW WE WORK | LAB | MISSION

ADD | TAGS | CATEGORIES | BOOKMARK & SHARE | META

S | ENTERTAINMENT | PREVIOUS / NEXT | LEARN MORE | T-SHIRTS

ERNS | PROMOTIONAL FLYER | MISSION STATEMENT | NETWORK

TEMAP | BUSINESS CLUB | STUDENTS | VISUALS | SYSTEM

VISIONARY IN RESIDENCE | DATING | XL | RULES | HOBBY

CREATE | PARTICIPATE | COOL GADGETS | RANKING

H ECK MESSAGES | MOVE | ACCESS | HIGHLIGHTS

CONDITIONS | POLICY | BECOME | MY PARTNER

S | REGISTER | SUBSCRIBE | TERMS OF USE | ESSAYS

TWITTER | SIGN IN | BUY NOW | GUIDELINES | ALUMNI

AGENT | APPLICATIONS | LIBRARY | PRINT THIS PAGE

OR | PERSONAL SHOPPER | PRIVACY POLICY | CONTACT US

content

content

content

content

**Today your friend,
tomorrow the world**

**Today your friend,
tomorrow the world**

**Today your friend,
tomorrow the world**

**Today your friend,
tomorrow the world**

**Today your friend,
tomorrow the world**

**Today your friend,
tomorrow the world**

Everyone Is a Designer in the Age of Social Media presents the Choice Generation of 2010.
Looking back at the first edition of *Everyone Is a Designer* in 2000, when we proposed the idea of democratization of design, a decade later this programmatic statement has become reality.
We are designing our social lives, make our own choices, and create it all together! This book signals a new aesthetic movement of collaborism: a combination of socially, technologically and economically driven systematically generated visuals.
A hierarchy of levels and layers, pull-down menus, buttons and blogrolls that give us access and possibilities to create visuals using style sheets, templates, renderings and frameworks for the look & feel of today's design.

Mieke Gerritzen & Geert Lovink

THE NEED FOR ARTISTIC SOFTWARE

[A MANIFESTO 1.0]

PROFESSIONAL DESIGNERS ARE LOOKING FOR A METAPOSITION SO THEY CAN PERFORM THEIR FUNCTION AS LEADERS.

Today, untrained designers and artists are also making films, photography and printed matter and developing products, and this has consequences for professional designers. Consumers can use affordable packages like Photoshop, InDesign and Flash to produce images. The designing masses could be guided if the range of software was considerably expanded and an artistic software suppliers' market arose alongside traditional art supply stores.

THE ARTISTIC PROPERTIES OF CODES AND SYSTEMS ARE BEING DISCOVERED!

Artists who once stomped their feet in paint can now break their brains with experimental coding experiences. Artistic software is slowly proliferating. It isn't technicians and monopoly holders like Adobe that will stimulate the development of special software but designers themselves, who are coming to seriously view code and computer languages as artists' materials. The culture of automatically generated images is still in its infancy.

remember
THE TOOLS

OK

MOVEMENT ▶	AMATEURS
OBJECT ◀	ART DECO
	AVANT GARDE
	BAUHAUS
FORM ◀	BUREAUCRATISM
	CHANGE
SHAPE ◀	COLLABORISM
	COMMERCIALISM
CONCEPT ◀	CRADLE TO CRADLE
	EVERYONE
	DATAVIS
RHETORIC ◀	DARK MARKETS
	FAVELA CHIC
PRINT ◀	FLUXUS
	GLAMORISM
CATEGORY ◀	**GOTHIC HIGH TECH**
	iHYPE
STYLE ◀	INFO-DECO
	MOBILE-MINDED
	MONALISING
MEDIA ◀	MODERNISM
	NEXT NATURE
CRITIC ◀	PICT SOCIETY
	POCHE
	POP ART
	POST-CANON
	POST-HUMAN
	POST-MODERNISM
	POST-TECHNO
	POWERPOINTLESS
	PUNK
	RADICALISM
	SOFT ARCHITECTURE
	SLOW
	TECHNO
	WILD SYSTEMS
	WIKIMEDIA

TEMPORARY IMAGE PRODUCTION BECOMES A SOCIAL ACTIVITY WHICH IS MOSTLY ABOUT COLLABORATION.

▼ SCREEN COMMUNICATION

We live in a media society that has become dependent on communication and network technology. We communicate mainly through screens, which are fed by more and more people, e.g., with photos on Flickr ("Share your photos. Watch the world.") and videos on YouTube ("Broadcast Yourself").

▼ VISUAL PRODUCTION

Countless people are now posting and creating visuals on the Internet; for these amateurs, graphic software for editing images is now supplied free, when buying a computer or camera, and sometimes its already installed on your new mobile phone. Visual production becomes part of the consumer industry and the new amateur designer see designing as choosing between templates and software.

▼ BORDERS DISAPPEAR

Bloggers call themselves curators, graphic designers become software developers, journalists become designers. Everyone is a photographer. Cultural disciplines as we knew them are changing and the borders between them are disappearing.

▼ THE PROFESSIONAL WORLD

The question is what the explosive growth of artistic production on the Internet means to the professional world of art and design.

▶ WORKING FOR GOOGLE

▶ SHARING KNOWLEDGE

SOMETIMES TO MAKE SOMETHING IS REALLY TO MAKE NOTHING;

and, paradoxically,

SOMETIMES TO MAKE NOTHING IS TO MAKE SOMETHING.

Quote from Francis Alÿs on his work "Paradox of Praxis" (1997), in which he pushed a block of ice through the streets of Mexico until it melted. Found by Sophie Krier.

▼ CREATIVITY FOR ALL

It doesn't matter if you have a degree from the Rhode Island School of Design or if you're a grandma in Tennessee with a bunch of free time and Adobe Illustrator. If the client likes the grandma's work better, then she's going to get the job. CHRISTOPHER STEINER, THE CREATIVITY OF CROWDS, FORBES.COM

▼ HOMO UNIVERSALIS

There are almost no specialists any more. Homo universalis 2.0 is in fact not just one person but several at once, linked by the network. MARIËTTE DÖLLE

▶ INTERNET

▼ DESIGN DISCOURSE

As the design discourse opens up, professional designers will shape the discourse by creating better and better tools and environments for public communication. (I am speaking here primarily of graphic design.) The biggest challenge facing all the design fields is the global environment. How can we create objects, systems, places, and tools that will help reverse the degradation of the world? This challenge, too, demands that the public be involved. The problem can't be solved by designers alone, but requires changes in how people live. ELLEN LUPTON

▼ PARTICIPATION

Understanding digital culture takes place by operating in that digital culture.

When **EVERYONE** becomes a designer, there are no middle-class consumers.

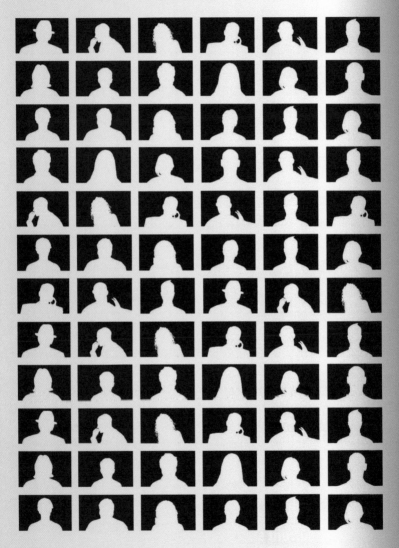

There's no mass market left. Modern people are torn between *Gothic High Tech* and *Favela Chic.*

GOTHIC HIGH TECH

GOTHIC HIGH TECH IS A *STARCHITECTURE WORLD*

IT'S GLORIOUS, GLAMOROUS, AND PROBABLY BROKE.

> THERE ARE SCARY, BLACKLY GAPING HOLES IN ITS POLITICAL AND ECONOMIC UNDERPINNINGS.

Vital working parts of Gothic High Tech have been off-shored, its employees decimated. The original planners of its superb schemes are retired, fired, fled or not legally liable for its current situation. It is wholly owned by weird, troubled, haunted global moguls.

FAVELA CHIC

Favela Chic is open-source and made from web instructions. It is young and cheap, but ignorant and superstitious. It lacks safety inspections or health regulations. If the shack-like structures of Favela Chic collapse and harm you, that is entirely your fault; it says so in the shrink-wrap, which you and its authors never read. You democratically followed your friends into Favela Chic. It never advertises, it leaves no paper trail. Like warm, flea-bitten kittens in a basket, Favela Chic costs nothing. We are incessantly told what Gothic High Tech should look like. No one believes in it. Nobody knows what well-designed Favela Chic looks like. No one asks that question.

done

THE WORLD IS URBANIZING AT ITS FASTEST RATE IN HISTORY, AND HAS JUST CROSSED THE 50% THRESHOLD.

Now, and for the foreseeable future, most of us will live in cities, and the fastest growing parts of the world's new cities are slums, built perforce by their inhabitants.

Put another way, the percentage of the world's people living in a designed environment is rising, but the percentage of the designed world created by trained designers is falling.

WHAT ARE THE CONCEPTS OF THE WORLD'S LEADING DESIGNERS?

THIS CREATES A CRISIS OF ACCESS;

like literacy after the printing press, design is becoming too important to leave to a cloistered few. For design to become more relevant in a world like this, we must find ways of expanding design practice to amateurs and to communal practice.

There is simply no way to scale or stretch a professional class of designers to cover the current need.

DONATE YOUR WISDOM TO THE CROWDS.

GENERATE
CONTENT

OK

▶ ACCESS

▼ CREATIVE MASS

The exclusive and valuable identity of design and the designer of the past century is replaced by a creative mass who uses the free design tools and worldwide networks to be part of the designed world.

▼ AMATEUR PROFESSIONAL

Passionate amateurs, using new tools, are creating products and paradigms that companies can't.
CHARLES LEADBEATER, 'THE RISE OF THE AMATEUR PROFESSIONAL'

▶ YOU ARE NOT A GADGET JARON LANIER

▼ GATEKEEPERS

As the old mass media industries of television, newspapers, book publishing, recorded music and movies teeter on the edge of collapse, it has become clear that the early 21st century digital revolution is having as profound an impact upon the gatekeepered culture industry as the mid 19th century industrial revolution had on society as a whole. ANDREW KEEN

TECHNOLOGY IS THE DRIVING FORCE

▶ MOVE TO NEXT LEVEL

I LOVE YOU

► CREATIVE COMMONS

► MORE FRIENDS

► FREE SOFTWARE

▼ FORGOT YOUR PASSWORD

The most common password among the 32 million people whose accounts were hacked at RockYou is '123456,' followed by '12345,' '123456789' and 'Password'. 'iloveyou' came in at no. 5. (IMPERVA.COM)

▼ UPLOADING

Humans are unique in their capacity not only to make tools, but to then turn around and use them to create superfluous material goods – painting, sculpture and architecture – and superfluous experiences – music, stories, religion, philosophy. Of course, it is precisely this superfluous uploading that defines human culture and ultimately what it is to be human. PETER LUNENFELD

▼ DOWNLOADING

All animals download, but only a few upload anything besides excrement and their own bodies. Beavers build dams, birds make nests, and termites create mounds, but for the most part, the animal kingdom moves through the world downloading, and then munching it bits at a time. PETER LUNENFELD

► FOLLOWERS

► RANKING

► BLOGGING

The Button is for fun, of course, but should highlight rather than hide the significance of our various *Whatever* moments. Buttons can be serious enough: consider the economic importance of Amazon's One-Click service. Or the implications of the many license agreements we click through so quickly. Given this, perhaps the *Whatever Button* can be used as an experiment for reflection. Are you careful with your data, avoiding ugly Third-Party clauses and monstrous Spyware? Or do you throw caution to the wind, opening up the personal information floodgates?
What button fits you best?

WHATEVER   CANCEL

▶ GOOGLE WORKERS

▼ WHATEVERBUTTON.COM

At almost every turn on the Web, we are asked to say yes. Yes to registration, yes to membership, yes to personal recommendations. Yes is said for us, with pre-filled checkboxes that read 'Keep me informed'. Or there might only be a semblance of choice - for example, saying no to browser cookies makes navigating the Web nearly impossible. More generally, however, it is a matter of clicking through the various forms in order to get what we want and to get to it faster. A matter of saying, 'Whatever'. And when that happens, we might wonder to what extent 'Yes' is our own default setting rather than that of the machine.

▼ DEMOCRAZY

Technology is changing how we look at art and how we make it. Everyone now uses the same tools to express themselves - artists and designers but also politicians and the public. Everyone produces and publishes text, video and photography. The arts are being fully democratised. Reflection and criticism of the world are thereby becoming part of a consumer industry.

▶ THE REAL WORLD

▼ STATUS

Amateurs have demonstrated in staggeringly diverse ways that low-production-quality work can nonetheless bear culturally important meanings ...

▶ COPYRIGHT

A4

A6

A5

A6

▶ **TECHNOLOGY**

▼ **OUR WORLD**

The world is covered by a tissue of standards that restructures the way we call it 'our world'. The new 'we' is determined by what is going to be our next common standard. Joining standards is like speaking languages. The way a Buy button sits on a web page is a PhD-level research topic. The next question is where the Vote button will be. A political scientist said that the choice between Chirac and Jospin in the 2002 French elections was like choosing between Coke and Pepsi. The question is whether and how we will allow ourselves to make the better choices with the best possible default settings. METAHAVEN

▶ **OPEN SOURCE**

▶ **OPEN STANDARDS FOR ALL**

▶ **TECHNO-ECONOMY**

▶ **72 DPI**

▶ **300 DPI**

▶ **GENERATED VISUALS**

▶ **DEN**

▶ **WIKI**

WHO SETS THE STANDARD?

FF 00 33	FF FF 00	FF 00 FF	00 CC FF	33 CC 00	33 33 CC	CC FF FF	99 00 33	99 99 99	CC FF FF	66 99 99	FF FF CC	00 CC FF	CD FE DE	33 33 CC
00 CC FF	FF 00 33	FF FF 00	FF 00 FF	00 CC FF	33 CC 00	33 33 CC	CC FF FF	66 66 66	FF 00 33	E6 E8 D0	FF 00 FF	99 CC CC	F0 E8 C2	D4 ED FF
FF 00 33	FF FF 00	FF 00 FF	00 CC FF	33 CC 00	33 33 CC	CC FF FF	99 00 33	99 99 99	CC FF FF	66 99 99	FF FF CC	00 CC FF	CD FE DE	33 33 CC
00 CC FF	FF 00 33	FF FF 00	FF 00 FF	00 CC FF	33 CC 00	33 33 CC	CC FF FF	66 66 66	FF 00 33	E6 E8 D0	FF 00 FF	99 CC CC	F0 E8 C2	D4 ED FF
FF 00 33	FF FF 00	FF 00 FF	00 CC FF	33 CC 00	33 33 CC	CC FF FF	99 00 33	99 99 99	CC FF FF	66 99 99	FF FF CC	00 CC FF	CD FE DE	33 33 CC
00 CC FF	FF 00 33	FF FF 00	FF 00 FF	00 CC FF	33 CC 00	33 33 CC	CC FF FF	66 66 66	FF 00 33	E6 E8 D0	FF 00 FF	99 CC CC	F0 E8 C2	D4 ED FF
FF 00 33	FF FF 00	FF 00 FF	00 CC FF	33 CC 00	33 33 CC	CC FF FF	99 00 33	99 99 99	CC FF FF	66 99 99	FF FF CC	00 CC FF	CD FE DE	33 33 CC
00 CC FF	FF 00 33	FF FF 00	FF 00 FF	00 CC FF	33 CC 00	33 33 CC	CC FF FF	66 66 66	FF 00 33	E6 E8 D0	FF 00 FF	99 CC CC	F0 E8 C2	D4 ED FF
FF 00 33	FF FF 00	FF 00 FF	00 CC FF	33 CC 00	33 33 CC	CC FF FF	99 00 33	99 99 99	CC FF FF	66 99 99	FF FF CC	00 CC FF	CD FE DE	33 33 CC
00 CC FF	FF 00 33	FF FF 00	FF 00 FF	00 CC FF	33 CC 00	33 33 CC	CC FF FF	66 66 66	FF 00 33	E6 E8 D0	FF 00 FF	99 CC CC	F0 E8 C2	D4 ED FF
FF 00 33	FF FF 00	FF 00 FF	00 CC FF	33 CC 00	33 33 CC	CC FF FF	99 00 33	99 99 99	CC FF FF	66 99 99	FF FF CC	00 CC FF	CD FE DE	33 33 CC
00 CC FF	FF 00 33	FF FF 00	FF 00 FF	00 CC FF	33 CC 00	33 33 CC	CC FF FF	66 66 66	FF 00 33	E6 E8 D0	FF 00 FF	99 CC CC	F0 E8 C2	D4 ED FF
FF 00 33	FF FF 00	FF 00 FF	00 CC FF	33 CC 00	33 33 CC	CC FF FF	99 00 33	99 99 99	CC FF FF	66 99 99	FF FF CC	00 CC FF	CD FE DE	33 33 CC
00 CC FF	FF 00 33	FF FF 00	FF 00 FF	00 CC FF	33 CC 00	33 33 CC	CC FF FF	66 66 66	FF 00 33	E6 E8 D0	FF 00 FF	99 CC CC	F0 E8 C2	D4 ED FF
FF 00 33	FF FF 00	FF 00 FF	00 CC FF	33 CC 00	33 33 CC	CC FF FF	99 00 33	99 99 99	CC FF FF	66 99 99	FF FF CC	00 CC FF	CD FE DE	33 33 CC

WE SHARE YOUR IDEAS!

DESIGN IS THE NEW SCIENCE

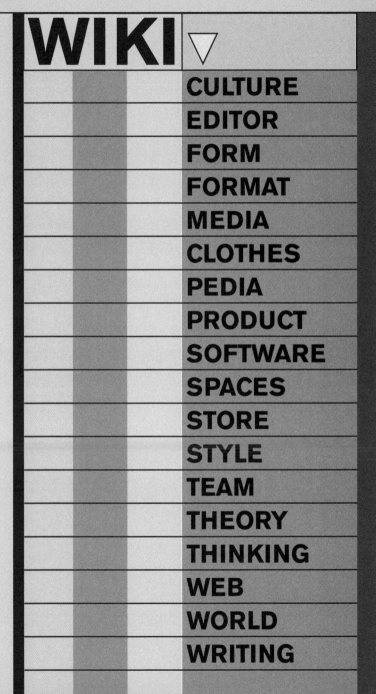

WIKI ▽

- CULTURE
- EDITOR
- FORM
- FORMAT
- MEDIA
- CLOTHES
- PEDIA
- PRODUCT
- SOFTWARE
- SPACES
- STORE
- STYLE
- TEAM
- THEORY
- THINKING
- WEB
- WORLD
- WRITING

Design is the planning that lays the basis for the making of every object or system. As a verb, "to design" refers to the process of originating and developing a plan for a product, structure, system, or component with intention. As a noun, "a design" is used for either the final (solution) plan (e.g. proposal, drawing, model, description) or the result of implementing that plan in the form of the final product of a design process. This classification aside, in its broadest sense no other limitations exist and the final product can be anything from clothing to graphical user interfaces to skyscrapers. Even virtual concepts such as corporate identity and cultural traditions such as celebration of certain holidays are sometimes designed. More recently, processes (in general) have also been treated as products of design, giving new meaning to the term "process design." The person designing is called a designer, which is also a term used for people who work professionally in one of the various design areas, usually also specifying which area is being dealt with (such as a fashion designer, concept designer or web designer). Designing often requires a designer to consider the aesthetic, functional, and many other aspects of an object or a process, which usually requires considerable research, thought, modeling, interactive adjustment, and redesign. With such a broad definition, there is no universal language or unifying institution for designers of all disciplines. This allows for many differing philosophies and approaches toward the subject. However, serious study of design demands increased focus on the design process. Design is the planning that lays the basis for the making of every object or system. As a verb, "to design" refers to the process of originating and developing a plan for a product, structure, system, or component.

This page in other languages

(als)	(ia)	(pam)
(ar)	(id)	(pl)
(be-tarask)	(it)	(pt)
(bg)	(ja)	(pt-br)
(bn)	(jv)	(ro)
(ca)	(ka)	(ru)
(cs)	(km)	(sk)
(da)	(ko)	(sv)
(de)	(ksh)	(ta)
(en)	(lb)	(te)
(el)	(lt)	(tr)
(eo)	(mk)	(tt)
(es)	(mr)	(uk)
(eu)	(ms)	(ur)
(fi)	(mt)	(vi)
(fr)	(bokmål)	(yue)
(gl)	(nb)	(zh-hans)
(hi)	(ne)	(zh-hant)
(hr)	(nl)	
(hu)	(oc)	

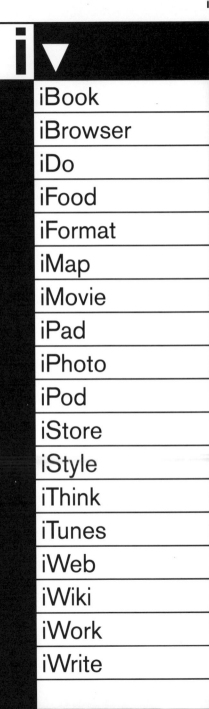

i ▼

iBook

iBrowser

iDo

iFood

iFormat

iMap

iMovie

iPad

iPhoto

iPod

iStore

iStyle

iThink

iTunes

iWeb

iWiki

iWork

iWrite

Design
EUROPE

OK

▼ DIGITAL NATIVES

A new generation of professional artists and designers is coming of age, a generation that grew up with internet, mobile telephones and virtual worlds. Technology is for them a fundamental component of their culture and identity. DAVID NIEBORG

▼ AUTHORSHIP

Authorship has thus made way for global cooperation, in which it is not the designers that take a central and decisive position, but instead it is an interesting theme or project that generates familiarity and fame.

▼ CAPITAL

The fundamental fact of modernity is no longer the earth circling around the sun but capital encircling the earth. We're the united colors of design. The one world of many cultures. We are the message of the media in cultural capitalism. HENK OOSTERLING

▼ NEW CONNECTIONS

Design represents social, aesthetic, political and geographical links that have arisen through technological developments.

► PLANET CULTURE

► MOBILITY

► DESIGN NOMADS

► DISTRIBUTION

Delete

BORDERS

○

○

○

OK

► RECOGNITION

▼ CHANGE

Technology is important because it empowers people. That's where you start. Not in novelty or neatness, not in the fact that it changes things, because it might change things by disempowering. Change is not in itself a valid reason for anything. DAVE WINER

▼ BORDERS

Are there mobile borders?

▼ IN BETWEEN

International networks, new media and globalisation have caused graphic design to enter the broad spectrum of visual culture. Graphic design has become a kind of in-between area. The Internet and network technology have completely changed the way we communicate, campaign and publicise.

THERE ARE NO LIMITS IN TECHNOLOGY

▼ INFORMATION

The conceptual media-conscious designer realises information is the basis for everything on earth.

Look
at my
decision!

DECIDED™

CATEGORY	▶
OBJECT	◀
FORM	◀
MOVEMENT	◀
CONCEPT	◀
RHETORIC	◀
BOOK TITLE	◀
CATEGORY	◀
STYLE	◀
MEDIA	◀
CRITIC	◀

ALGORITHM DESIGN
AMATEUR DESIGN
ANARCHIST DESIGN
ARCHITECTURAL DESIGN
BACK-END DESIGN
BALLOON DESIGN
BODY DESIGN
CORPORATE DESIGN
CRITICAL DESIGN
DESIGN EXTENSION
DESIGN DELIGHT
DESIGN ON DEMAND
DESIGN FOR DEBATE
DASEIN IS DESIGN
EVOLUTIONARY DESIGN
FOOD DESIGN
FUNCTIONAL DESIGN
FUNDAMENTAL DESIGN
FREE-RANGE DESIGN
HOLISTIC DESIGN
INDUSTRIAL DESIGN
INTELLIGENT DESIGN
INTERFACE DESIGN
LOW RES DESIGN
MODERNIST DESIGN
NETWORK DESIGN
ORGANIC DESIGN
OFF DESIGN
POWERPOINT DESIGN
PRINT DESIGN
PRODUCT DESIGN
RELIGIOUS DESIGN
SOFTWARE DESIGN
SLOW DESIGN
SERIOUS DESIGN
SYMBOL DESIGN
TECHNO DESIGN
WALLPAPER DESIGN

DESIGN EXISTENTIALISM

'Design your own life' seems to be the ultimate maxim that expresses the extension of design practice from mere objects to the existential design of life itself. It's the slogan of an advertisement campaign by IKEA ▼

THE ADAPTATION OF SARTRE'S NOTION THAT

MAN IS NOTHING ELSE BUT WHAT HE MAKES OF HIMSELF - and one cannot

imagine a more appropriate place to launch such a statement.

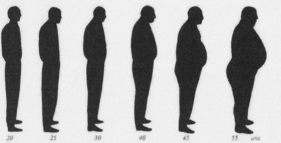

20   25   30   40   45   55   *ans*

IVAR
BILL
INTR
TRAI
STO
NIAN

In the temple of the democratization of design, and in a time of near ubiquity of design objects, desire for originality and exclusivity moves to the next level. It assumes the destruction of the 'aura' of the design object, its uniqueness replaced by a

SENSE OF THE UNIVERSAL EQUALITY OF THINGS,
guaranteed by mass reproduction and ultimately

(The horror! The horror!),
the object's appearance in an IKEA catalogue.

iedereen = designer

The design object, stripped of its authenticity-through-scarcity, becomes a mere instrument, through which that other 'aura' is obtained: the coveted faculties of the designers themselves:

CREATIVITY, ORIGINALITY, BOHEMIAN LIFE-STYLE, A CERTAIN HINT OF GENIUS; THOSE MARKS OF DISTINCTION THAT ALLOW ONE TO DESIGN ONE'S LIFE WITH A FEELING OF FALSE AUTHENTICITY.

Whereas before this was true for a small minority, its delusion is now democratic.

Repent! Repent!
The end is near...
BY MERIJN OUDENAMPSEN

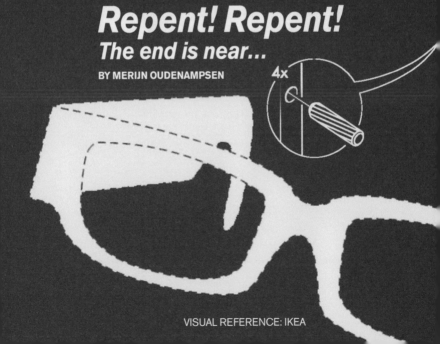

VISUAL REFERENCE: IKEA

DESIGN MEANS MORE CHAOS

THE TOTAL EXPERIENCE MANAGEMENT OF EVERYTHING

from the arrangement of flat percentiles of fields of vision to that of social interactions is one of high quality control. In such a world, every task must be subsumed into something with all the procedural thrills of a tax form, but one that triggers your emotions or wins your allegiance, while making sure to take down your details. Against the subsumption architecture of life as it ought to be, in its sustainable, experiential, or efficiency-enhancing forms, comes the bleak comic art of random deletions, extra-complicated business, orderly sequences of well-defined instructions that bulge out into billowing clouds of life-draining optimisations. Working in between these two is the work of the designer, the worm that secretes the book, the moth that makes clothes, wind that secretes instruments. To design today means to make patient chaos against both the paradise of simplification and the computationally-enhanced, market-ready complications of smartness. Design is the glorious hole in the bagel, feast on it.

▼ OVERLOAD

The Principle of Engagement: we must work through protocol, not against it. ALEX GALLOWAY

▼ WHAT WE ARE

We are no longer the reasonable, thinking beings which modernist design tried to make us into.
METAHAVEN

▼ MEDIA

The twentieth century will be remembered as that time when all was not media. ALEX GALLOWAY

▼ PRAXIS

The only good design is design that enhances the possibilities for praxis. Praxis is the capacity to collectively know and transform our world. Praxis is neither working nor playing, hacking nor hustling. All of these are just fragments of a capacity yet to come into being. Praxis is that which our separate currently existing activities reveal as possible but fettered by current modes of power and property. Design can either make a contribution to the creation of the possibility of praxis, or it can go through the motions of redecorating the cabin of the zeppelin while it crashes. Safe travels, designers. MCKENZIE WARK

▼ YOUR CHOICE

Feel free to reject my invitation. GEERT LOVINK

▼ QUALITY

Failure is overrated. STEFAN SAGMEISTER

Media is becoming highly visual and objects around us are in turn becoming media.

▼ INFORMATION SOCIETY

Our surroundings used to be made up of things; in the future, they will be made up of information. We no longer only see shop advertising, traffic signs and billboards as informative images; buildings, cars, high-speed trains, airports and clothing are now also objects of information. KOERT VAN MENSVOORT

▼ VISUAL INFLATION

Facebook and Twitter are the most popular forms of communication.

▼ DATA VISUALISATION

Data visualisation is the study of the visual representation of data, meaning "information which has been abstracted in some schematic form, including attributes or variables for the units of information." WIKIPEDIA, 14-03-2010

▼ NEW-STYLE COMMUNICATION

The new form – the visualisation of moving information – allows one to make serious information accessible in an attractive manner. Until about ten years ago, people saw text as the logical way of sharing information; today, audiovisual is the norm, preferably in an atmosphere of entertainment. FRANK KALSHOVEN AND MARTIJN BENNIS, DE NIEUWE REPORTER

▼ INFOVIS FOR JOURNALISTS

Journalists should experiment more with new information visualisation techniques. The old adage "Form follows function" applies here. BAS BROEKHUIZEN, DE NIEUWE REPORTER

form follows
FORMAT

OK

▶ VISUAL CULTURE

▼ HOMO INFORMANS

Our behaviour is shaped by the beat of the media, the murderous tempo of everyday medio-crity. In post-mortal manner: from one broken deadline to the next. Our lives have become radically medio-cre in this zombie-esque frenzy. We live the life of homo informans. That's right, not homo sapiens, but homo informans - which brings us to the first shift in the triangle: knowledge is information, facts are pure data. HENK OOSTERLING

▼ COMPLEX INFORMATION

We are developing a zap-like, non-linear way of thinking, which allows us to absorb highly complex information. KOERT VAN MENSVOORT

INFORMATION DESIGN IS:
COMPLEXITY
INTERDISCIPLINARITY
EXPERIMENT

▶ THE RISE OF DATA SOAPS

Remember
OLD MEDIA

OK

Designer Software outlet!

DESIGNED™

BEWARE OF SOFTWARE

IMAGE INSPIRED BY KLAUS STAECK'S *VORSICHT KUNST*

© *image of worker: nobodyhere.com*

▶ **MEDIA**

▶ **SYSTEMS**

▶ **NETWORK**

▼ **SOFTWARE**

Software has already become a big part of culture - with hundreds of thousands of people writing it and millions of people discussing it. LEV MANOVICH

MAKE YOUR COMPUTER A REAL DESIGNER

WITH THE SOFTWARE YOU FIND HERE! *[EMAIL SPAM]*

▶ **LEARNING FROM CODE**

▼ **HISTORY**

Most filters in programs are based on techniques, effects and visual styles that were thought up in the past for old media.

Back-end Beauty!

CMS
STYLE

FOR BETTER DESIGN DECISIONS

▼ FILTERS (DANGER)

By our own very nature we filter, forget, hear, and see selectively, but that doesn't mean that we have to agree with all the filtering done on our behalf.
GEERT LOVINK

▼ THE DESIGN POSITION

If the designer wants the meta position, he or she will become a software designer who develops cool tools for the crowd.

► EFFECTS

▼ FILTERS (INVISIBILITY)

The danger of filters is their invisibility. What we need is a growing awareness of the existence and architecture of the filters that surround us. GEERT LOVINK

▼ FILTERS (FAILURE)

The problem is filter failure, not information overload, Clay Shirky once stated. I would rephrase this: it is the lack of awareness of the filter architecture that produces the feeling of information overload. GEERT LOVINK

THE THINGS WE DESIGN END UP DESIGNING US

► USER GENERATED DESIGN

Choose for
BIO-IMAGERY

- ○ twitter
- ○ You Tube
- ○ flickr

OK

▶ NANO

▼ BIO-IMAGERY

It has all become evolutionary. Human beings find it difficult to set limits and, in our current consumer society, are constantly struggling to retain control. We have already analysed food, traffic and the environment; now it is the turn of the image culture. Is there such a thing as a bio-image? Or a free-range image? An image that has been given the time to develop? Time to create a context? Something that can be processed by well-trained image workers?

▼ NOOSPHERE

Designs that celebrate the noosphere tend to energize the inner troll or bad actor within humans.
JARON LANIER

▶ NEXT NATURE

▼ INTERACTION

Anonymous blog comments, vapid video pranks, and lightweight mashups may seem trivial and harmless, but as a whole, this widespread practice of fragmentary, impersonal communication has demeaned interpersonal interaction. JARON LANIER

▼ THE WORLD

The ocean is made-to-order businessware and a place for economic growth. KOERT VAN MENSVOORT

▶ SLOW IMAGES

RAZORIUS GILLETTUS
On the Origin of the Next Species

INNOVATION

My first razor I got when I was fifteen. It consisted of two blades on a simple metal stick and I remember it gave me a really close and comfortable shave. In the twenty years that have passed since my first shave, I've used seven different models of razors. This morning I shaved myself with the Gillette Fusion Power Phantom, a rather heavy, yet ergonomically designed battery-powered razor that looks like a bit like a vacuum cleaner and has five vibrating blades with an aloe strip for moisture. So what happened?

THIS IS A STORY ABOUT DESIGN, TECHNOLOGY, MARKET AND EVOLUTION. →

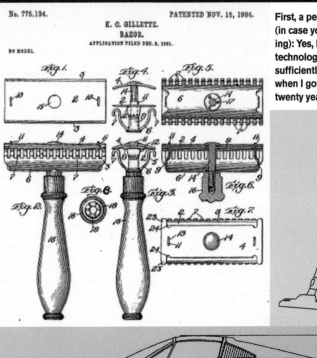

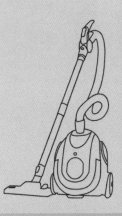

First, a personal disclaimer (in case you were wondering): Yes, I agree shaving technology was already sufficiently developed when I got my first razor twenty years ago (1989).

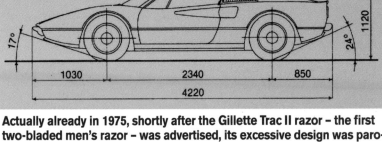

Actually already in 1975, shortly after the Gillette Trac II razor – the first two-bladed men's razor – was advertised, its excessive design was parodied on the US television show Saturday Night Live. The creators of the satirical television programme played on the notion of a two-bladed razor as a sign of the emerging consumption culture and made a fake commercial parody for a fictitious razor with the ridiculous number of three (!) blades, emphasising the consumer is gullible enough to believe and buy everything seen on TV. Of course, the comedians of Saturday Night Live could not know a three-bladed razor would become a reality on the consumer market in the late 1990s. Let alone could they have anticipated I would shave with a five-bladed razor this very morning.

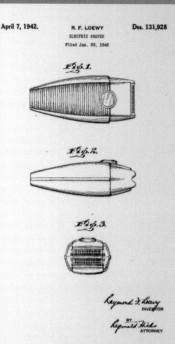

April 7, 1942.   R. F. LOEWY   Des. 131,928
ELECTRIC SHAVER
Filed Jan. 29, 1942

Fig.1.

Fig.2.

Fig.3.

Raymond F. Loewy
INVENTOR
BY
Reginald Hicks
ATTORNEY

Fortunately, it is still possible to buy brand new blades for my very first razor model today. These older blades are not only cheaper – they are sold in a box of ten for less money than a box of blades fitting the latest model, which contains only four cassettes. The older blades are also more durable. And yet, in the years that have passed since my first shave, I've bought over a dozen different razors – I honestly have to confess I've bought some models of the competing brand as well.

Welcome to the twenty-first century: No, we don't travel in spaceships… but we do have five-bladed razors!

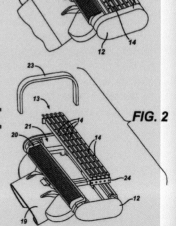

FIG. 1

FIG. 2

So, why did I buy the whole collection of razors over the years? Perhaps it is because I am the type of person who is keen on new things:

I AM A SUCKER FOR INNOVATION!

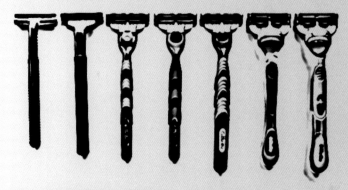

COPY PASTE MIX
BREED DELETE
EVOLVE
Before we analyze my own behaviour as a buyer, let's first study the razors. If we look at the development of razor technology over time, we can distinguish quite a few similarities with an evolutionary development as we know from the biological world:

① *EVERY NEW MODEL* BUILDS UPON THE PROPERTIES OF THE PREVIOUS MODEL.

② SUCCESSFUL VARIANTS ARE PRESERVED IN FUTURE GENERATIONS, WHEREAS UNSUCCESSFUL VARIANTS WILL FADE OUT.

③ THE SHIFT FROM FUNCTIONAL TECHNOLOGIES, LIKE A PIVOTING HEAD, TO SEEMINGLY FUNCTIONLESS AESTHETICS OF THE NEWER MODELS, THAT ONLY CHANGE IN COLOUR AND HAVE NO OTHER PURPOSE THAN TO STAND OUT AMIDST THE COMPETING RAZOR MODELS, REMIND US OF THE EXUBERANT TAIL OF A MALE PEACOCK.

④ THE UNIQUE CLICK-ON SYSTEMS FOR REPLACEMENT BLADES ON DIFFERENT MODELS RESEMBLE BIOLOGICAL IMMUNE SYSTEMS WITHHOLDING INTRUDERS FROM ENTERING AND FEEDING ON YOUR ENVIRONMENT.

⑤ THERE EVEN ARE DIFFERENT SURVIVAL STRATEGIES BEING TESTED, WHICH OVER TIME MAY EVEN RESULT IN SEPARATE SPECIES – THINK OF THE PARALLEL BRANCHES IN THE MORE RECENT MODELS THAT COME WITH AND WITHOUT A BATTERY. APPARENTLY THE MARKETERS AREN'T SURE WHETHER ELECTRIC OR NON-ELECTRIC SHAVING IS THE FUTURE AND HAVE DECIDED TO GAMBLE ON BOTH STRATEGIES – AND YES, I CONFESS: I BOUGHT THEM BOTH.

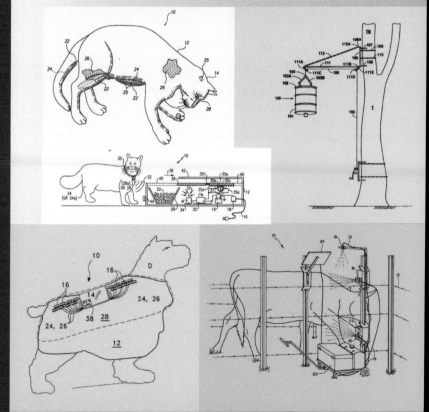

RAZORIUS GILLETTUS
On the Origin of the Next Species

ECONOMY

INTELLIGENT DESIGNER

Now it may seem quirky, corny even, to consider the development of razors from an evolutionary perspective. After all, these are industrial products assembled in factories. Yet I propose to look at them as the result of an evolutionary process. Now I already hear you arguing: "These razors didn't evolve, people designed them! How can that be an evolutionary process?" Well, let me elaborate – and this is where we learn something about our symbiotic relation with technology. Indeed it is true that all the individual razors were created by engineers and designers; however, if we look at the design of the whole series of shavers as it developed throughout my shaving career, it will be difficult to pinpoint one creator. Where is that one big mind, that 'intelligent designer' responsible for the transformation of the razor from a simple blade on a stick to a five-bladed electric razor?

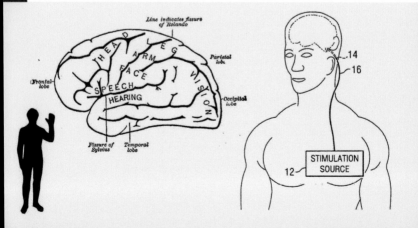

Obviously many designers and engineers have been involved in the creation of my razors over the years. No doubt these are all decent and friendly people – with good incomes too – but what more are these creators of the individual models than little cogs in the perpetuating Gillette Company? Calling them engineers and designers is arguably too much credit for the work they do, as they merely sketch the next razor model, of which one can already predict the 'innovative' new properties: it will be a slight variation on the current model with some added nanotech-sharpened blade, an extra moisture strip, an anti-slip grip or perhaps even a custom customizable colour scheme. The razor designers don't have a lot of room for truly creative design work, really.

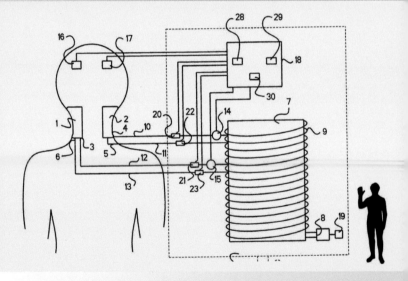

It's not like they are in a position to think deeply on the meaning and origins of shaving, in order to reinvent this ancient ritual. Like bees in a beehive, their work is determined by the logic of the larger structure.

The chair of that one great 'intelligent designer' steering the entire development of shavers over time is empty. The larger design gesture emerges from the closely interrelated forces of the consumer market, technological affordances and of course the competition – think of the Wilkinson brand that first introduced a four-bladed shaving system, thereby forcing Gillette to answer with a five-bladed system. Together these contextual influences constitute an ecosystem of a sort, which (again) closely resembles the environmental forces known to play a part in the evolutionary development of biological species.

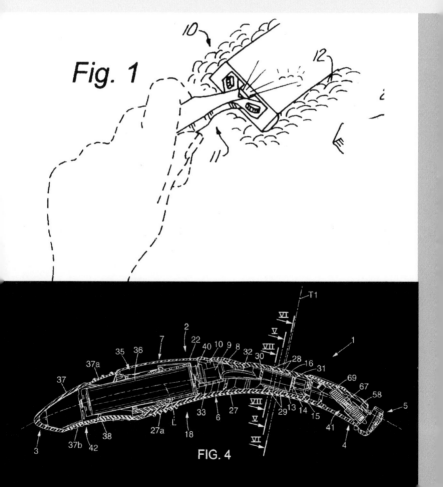

Fig. 1

FIG. 4

EVOLUTION
BUT NOT AS WE KNOW IT

Of course there are also arguments against this evolutionary view on the development of razor technology – so let's work at both sides of the coin here. The most common objection is that "people play a role in the process, so it can't be evolution."

This reasoning is tempting; however, it also positions people outside of nature – as if we are somehow placed outside of the game of evolution and its rules don't apply to us. There is no reason to believe this is the case: after all, people have evolved just like all other life. The fact that my razors are dependent on people to multiply is also not unprecedented. The same is valid nowadays for many domesticated fruits like bananas as well as a majority of the cattle on our planet. Moreover, we see similar symbiotic relationships in old nature: just think of the flowers that are dependent on bees to spread their seeds.

Another objection might be that my razors cannot be the result of an evolutionary development because they are made of metal and plastic and not a carbon-based biological species. Underneath this argument lies the assumption that evolution only takes place within a certain medium: carbon-based life forms. A variation of this argument states that evolution only takes place if there are genes involved – like with humans, animals and plants.

EVOLUTION TAKES PLACE WITHIN A CERTAIN MEDIUM: *CARBON-BASED LIFE FORMS.*

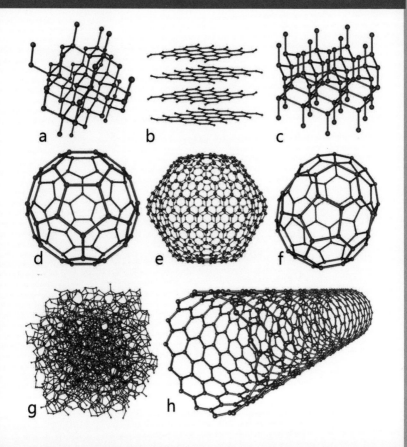

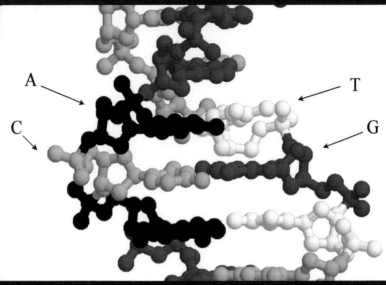

MEDIUM - PRINCIPLE

This way of thinking exemplifies a limited understanding of evolution, as it is a mistake to constrain it to a certain medium rather than to understand it as a principle. In fact, the genetic system of DNA underlying our species is itself also a product of evolution – DNA evolved from the simpler RNA system as a successful medium for coding life. There is no reason why evolutionary processes could not transfer themselves to other media:

> **RICHARD DAWKINS PROPOSED**
> # 'MEMES'
> **AS BUILDING BLOCKS OF**
> *CULTURAL EVOLUTION.*
>
> **SUSAN BLACKMORE SUGGESTED**
> # 'TEMES'
> **AS BUILDING BLOCKS FOR**
> *TECHNOLOGICAL EVOLUTION.*

In the end, the question we should ask ourselve is:

> **ARE THE ENVIRONMENTAL FORCES OF ECONOMY AND TECHNOLOGY, AT LEAST EQUALLY OR PERHAPS EVEN MORE IMPORTANT FOR THE SHAPING OF RAZOR TECHNOLOGY THAN THE DESIGN DECISIONS MADE BY THE 'INVENTORS' OF THE INDIVIDUAL MODELS?**

**I am pretty sure this is the case and hence I propose we consider the development of razors as a truly evolutionary process – not metaphorically, but in reality. The species it has brought into being we will call: RAZORIUS GILLETTUS.
It is just one of the numerous new species emerging within the techno-economic system – and it is evolving fast.**

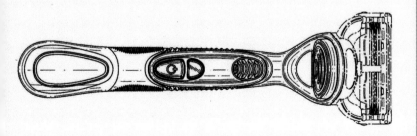

TECHNODIVERSITY IS INCREASING

Once we agree to perceive the development of razor technology as an evolutionary process, we can zoom in a bit on our own role in the evolutionary game.

How can we see our relationship with Razorius Gillettus and its numerous fellow evolving techno-species? Are we like the bees – who feed themselves with nectar from flowers and in return spread their pollen, enabling the flowers to reproduce – heading towards a symbiotic relationship with the technosphere, which feeds upon our labour and creativity, and in return gives us Razorius Gillettus?

Should we take pride in our role as catalysts of evolution? Propagators of a technodiversity unlike the world has ever seen: the one and only animal that transfers the game of evolution into another medium? We can. Yet, as in every symbiotic relationship, we should also be keen on both parties actually getting a good deal. And although I did buy all these razors and they have been providing me with an ever-smoother-closer shave throughout my life, I am not entirely sure about that.

RAZORIUS GILLETTUS
On the Origin of the Next Species

EVOLUTION

INNOVATION WITHOUT A CAUSE

To many of what we call 'innovations' are merely directed at increasing the growth and well-being of the technosphere – bigger economy, bigger corporations,more technological devices – rather than actually im-proving the lives of people. Indeed, my latest shaver does shave just that tiny little bit more smoothly than the previous model. Yet, if you asked me if the device had 'innovated' my life, I'd have to say no.

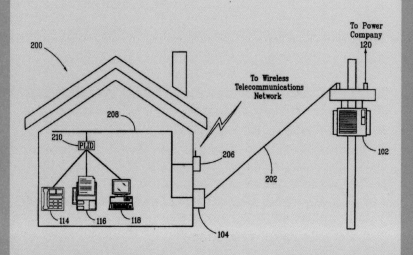

Let's face it: the new shavers from Gillette are primarily created for the sake of Gillette: higher turnover, more profit, more shareholder value. Now that's all not bad to begin with, as good business also provides people with good jobs and steady incomes, which allows them to live a happy life – and buy more razors. So far it's a win-win situation. Yet the production of all these abundant devices also uses an amazing amount of resources, putting great pressure on the biosphere – remember, that old nature that used to surround us before the emergence of the technosphere? We should not be naïve about the fact that corporations – I know they'll tell you otherwise – do not intrinsically care all that much about the wellbeing of the biosphere. Being able to breathe clean air simply is not important for Razorius Gillettus, as it has a whole different digestive system. Clean air is merely a requirement for carbon–based life forms like algae, plants, birds, polar bears, and of course people.

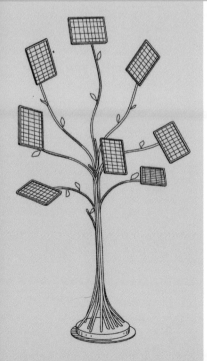
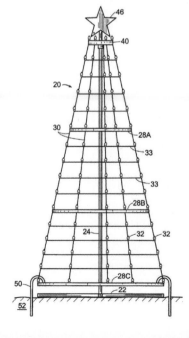

CATALYSTS OF EVOLUTION

So how to continue? I am the first to concur that there is a certain appeal to the development of Razorius Gillettus. The notion that human activity is causing the rising of such a peculiar new species and that we are now co-evolving towards a shared future is intriguing to say the least. I wonder what Charles Darwin would have thought of this. Perhaps he would have pointed at the serious risks involved in this evolutionary leap. Certainly, our awareness of our own role as 'catalysts of evolution' has yet to mature. It is a quite responsible job description we have got our hands on there. If we feel we are not fit for the job, we could better grow our beards and return to our caves. At least some people have proposed we should; however, trying to turn back the clock of civilization would also be a denial of what it means to be human, or at least exemplify a coward-liness towards the unknown. On the other hand, a purely techno-utopist attitude of 'letting things grow' will also not be in the longterm benefit of humanity and our fellow biosphere–dependent species, as we run the risk of being outsourced altogether.

TRYING TO TURN BACK THE CLOCK OF CIVILIZATION WOULD ALSO BE A DENIAL OF WHAT IT MEANS TO BE HUMAN

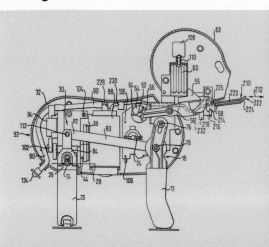

The mature thing to do in our position as catalysts of evolution is to develop a stewardship that focuses on maintaining a balance between both the declining biosphere and the emerging technosphere – between old nature and the next nature. Towards an environment in which both can find a place and live in relative harmony. Now, I am not saying it will be easy. But if we are able to do that, we will have something to be truly proud of.

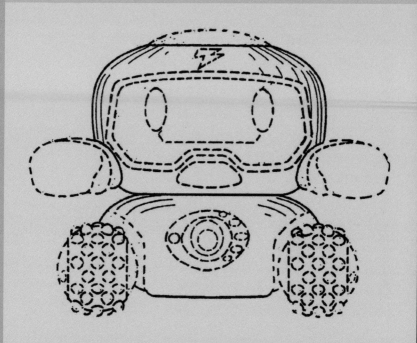

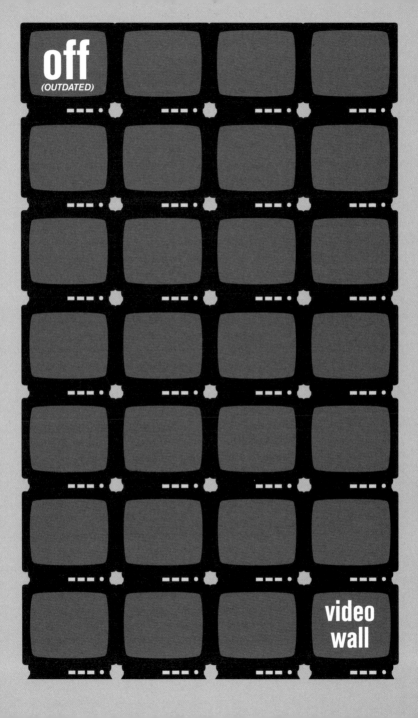

START YOUR OWN ▼

SUPERMARKET ◀

MUSEUM ◀

BUSINESS ◀

MASTER'S COURSE ◀

MOVEMENT ◀

PUBLISHING HOUSE ◀

BROADCAST STATION ◀

DESIGN OFFICE ◀

BANK ◀

NETWORK.ORG ◀

CORPORATION ◀

PHOTO SHOP
JAVA SCRIPT
LINKED IN
FACE BOOK
YOU TUBE
FREE HAND
KEY NOTE
POWER POINT
IN DESIGN
LIFE TYPE
QUICK TIME
DREAM WEAVER
FIRE WORKS
AFTER EFFECTS
MICRO SOFT
SOUND BOOTH

▼ LOGO LANGUAGE

If you look at the names, logos, and trademarks of social media companies, you see some remarkable parallels. Many of them are two words meshed up: Face + Book, You + Tube, Linked + In. Many are invented, fictional names: Skype, Vimeo, Flickr, Hyves, even Google. And many of their brightly coloured logos - lime green the new yellow, orange the new red, blue the new blue - are a far cry from what a trademark or emblem should look like according to the modernist heritage from the age of mass production. METAHAVEN

▶ LOGO SPHERE

▶ FROM CRADLE TO CAPITAL

RECOGNITION IS THE MOST SUCCESSFUL PRODUCT

▼ UNLIMITED

Design is a consumer good and there is no limit to consumption.

▼ AM I IN THE PICTURE?

For texting and Skyping screenagers, Am I in the picture? is a nonquestion. Located by GPS and face recognition, the young are constantly in touch with one another through Hyves, Facebook, and YouTube. The virtuality of this way of being, of this designed Dasein, can no longer be measured by the yardstick of history. HENK OOSTERLING

▼ KNOWLEDGE

The social media entrepreneurs and designers know something we don't know. METAHAVEN

WE ARE ALL GOLD FARMERS

▼ MARKETING STRATEGY

The Corporate Story is the research project of our business. The Corporate Story is not an artistic happening. A corporate story is not a journalistic product or report. It is an imaginative product in which credibility is more important than truth. Reality is created in word and image. WILLEM KOCH

MONALISING
THE WORLD

  by Leonardo Da Vinci

  by Shepard Fairley

  by Andy Warhol

OK

▼ MONALISING

The Mona Lisa is the most frequently reproduced work of art; the painting functions as a business model for the commercial operation of the Louvre. Monalising is a concept that links visual communication with the branding of art. Mass attachment to a product, object or event creates a connection and generates trust.

HOW TO TURN YOUR CREATIVITY INTO MONEY?

▼ CULTURAL MARKET

As well as cars, food and consumer goods, big corporations like to produce luxury items such as fashion, design, makeup and gadgets. These luxury products get compared with art; their purpose is the same. Cultural products are expensive and special: according to marketers, they lift our spirits and make us feel good. Our need to surround ourselves with these cultural products grows by the day. Subcultures and obscure views on life are suddenly dynamic factors in the economy. Cultural niches are becoming players on the financial market.

We are tired of rhizomes

TRIBE™

▼ LABOUR

The web is the world's largest sweatshop. ALEX GALLOWAY

▼ MARKET OF AESTHETICS

Design has transformed into an economic factor.

▼ CAPITAL

Capital wants us to be fat, distracted, indebted, whatever beings. As these beings, we become incapable of desiring something else or of conceiving of our desires as something we might realise collectively, with discipline and sacrifice. JODI DEAN

▼ POLITICS

Today, politics is falling under the influence of the consumer industry. Political conviction serves as input for brand development and cross-media branding. The politician is becoming a product and politicians travel the world like pop stars, their performances lighting up screens in all corners of the globe.

▼ ENVIRONMENT

Once, artists painted clouds and landscapes, because that was what they saw around them; today, their surroundings consist of the same logos, icons and familiar images everywhere.
Direct marketing and corporate identities now largely determine how the western streetscape looks.

▼ HIGH DATA

To demonstrate world-class expertise, avoid quickly written, shallow postings. Instead, invest your time in thorough, value-added content that attracts paying customers. JACOB NIELSEN

FORM FOLLOWS DATA

▼ VISUAL INFLATION

The rise of data is the waning of the visual.

▼ DATA MARKET

We need to distrust Google's intention to "organise the world's information" and see it as a worldwide move towards data manipulation, driven by a curious dynamic of state control and corporate interest. GEERT LOVINK

▼ DATA REVOLUTION

Science, business, government and many other fields are fully aware of the data revolution of the 2000s. Many scientific fields have been transformed by the availability of massive volumes of data and the ability to work on it computationally. LEV MANOVICH

SUPPORT MY EXIT

▼ AVANT GARDE

There has never been an avant garde of the algorithm. ALEX GALLOWAY

ALGORITHM-AIDED HUMAN WRITING WILL MEET HUMAN-AIDED ALGORITHMIC CURATION; *QUALITY WILL RISE!*

JEFF JARVIS, AUTHOR OF WHAT WOULD GOOGLE DO?

▼ COMPUTER

The new media are fundamentally sadistic, in that they construct worlds filled with manipulatable objects. ALEX GALLOWAY

▼ TRUST THE SYSTEM

Our lives are programmes; computerisation knows no bounds. Our traditions and behaviours are analysed and processed into standard software packages. Whether you want to distribute products, pre-programme a pizza oven, book a last-minute trip to Spain or even build a house, you can get a handy software package or access the necessary knowledge and information via an online service. On the one hand, these technological aids are a boon, saving us time, work and money; on the other, we are losing control over the systems; for example, viruses and spam are invading our computers. We regularly adapt our behaviours, and thus, in a manner of speaking, human action is controlled by technological systems.

THE GRAPHIC DESIGNER BECOMES A SOFTWARE DEVELOPPER

AFTER THE DEMOCRATISATION OF THE DESIGN DISCIPLINE, THE LEADING DESIGNER WILL BECOME A SOFTWARE DEVELOPER IF HE OR SHE WANTS TO EXPLORE THE PRODUCTION OF NEW CHARACTERISTIC IMAGES.

DESIGN CRITERIA FUTURE
LOVE IT OR LEAVE IT

DESIGNED BY PEOPLE

Where is the designer when design becomes automated by algorithms?

Will the next generation of designers come from the digital sweatshops piling up across Asia?

Is there an equivalent to attention deficit disorder that defines contemporary design cultures?

The impulse is to answer these last two questions in the affirmative and the implication of the first is that a programmed decisionism blows disciplinary borders into oblivion.

© *image: Gerd Arntz (1900-1988)*

WEB-GENERATED DESIGN SLOGANS PROVIDE AN INDEX OF INCOHERENCE THAT SIGNALS THE FUTURE-PRESENT OF DESIGN DISCIPLINES:

DESIGN CRITERIA FUTURE
LOVE IT OR LEAVE IT

WEB-GENERATED DESIGN SLOGAN: *KEEP GOING WELL, KEEP GOING QUALITY DESIGN CONTROL.* **There's a semblance of sense here, but not much more. The disarray of design grammar is at once refreshing and without foundation.**

THE AESTHETICS OF CONNECTION ACROSS TIME AND SPACE NO LONGER INSTITUTES THE HISTORY OF DESIGN AS WE KNOW IT, NO MATTER WHAT NATIONAL CULTURE YOU WISH TO IDENTIFY.

Tomorrow's designers have no sense of continuum. Their style is driven by affective desires and economic urgencies – two conflicting forces that hold their own distinct brutalities, but without guarantees for design futures. Since the academies are so questionable, the serious designer might fairly ask, 'where to then?' Eclecticism is rarely without interest and populates the streets with great abundance across the world. Translation is the key to post-disciplinary design.

PHOTOSHOP
RECOGNITION

OK

▼ IMAGE ECONOMY

The industrial developments of the 20th century have made way for irreversible technological developments. The technical possibilities of image are becoming increasingly advanced. Hardly a month passes by without a new product for an even better picture resolution appearing on the market. We are zooming ever closer in on the image and losing distance to the actual illustration. We are adrift in an image culture. Creativity is the driving power behind the western economy.

▼ MARKET OF AESTHETICS

Despite the growing attention for design in a network environment, online aesthetics are still poorly developed in comparison with the designs and the process of designing for the physical world.

DOWNLOAD THE VITAL VISUAL NOW

▼ LIFESTYLE

Daring logos and styles are meant to make us believe we're all connected.

On the internet you can now visit

MoOM

the Museum of Online Museums

AND SO...
THE MUSEUM ITSELF IS
BECOMING INCREASINGLY
SELF-REFLECTIVE AS IT
MOVES FROM THE DIDACTIC
THROUGH THE IMAGINARY TO
THE VIRTUAL.

▼ IMAGE CONSUMPTION

Visual culture has its limits. The constant need for pictures has led to a surfeit of images. It is like that with everything in this world. People are attracted to anything uncommon or rare; the ability to make nearly anything is causing an increase in rarity, which usually leads to overload. This is true with food, fashion, design and images.

DESIGN YOUR STRUGGLE

▼ THE POWER OF IMAGINATION

An image is dependent on the situation it is found in. Images are generated and constructed. In technological and digital development, the challenge is to create an image as dynamically and fully as possible, with maximum precision, preferably at a higher resolution than the eye can perceive. High-speed networks and advanced technologies ensure that images, visual culture and visualisation are becoming more important than physical visual existence.

► VIRAL MARKETING

SHAPING
THE PLANET

OK

▼ IMAGE-GENERATING AMATEURS

The danger of visual inflation lies largely in the mass of image-generating amateurs who have not the slightest knowledge of image culture. More and more products are appearing that deliver the required information in a made-to-measure way. The consumer no longer wishes to be served; he serves himself. Internet and network technology have totally changed our way of communicating, publishing and running campaigns. The growth of image production cannot be stemmed and the tools for making and consuming images - the gadgets - have become consumer products intended for stimulating the market.

WORLD'S LEAD-ING IMAGES ARE OBJECTS OF POWER

▼ DESIGN STUDENTS

Creativity is the driving power behind the western economy and everywhere design schools are springing up like mushrooms. But do we have the capabilities for training those thousands of design students properly?

Menu and content dynamic

Menu fixed, content dynamic

Menu and content dynamic

3 columns all dynamic

4 columns all dynamic

Menu floating

Menu fixed, content & header dynamic

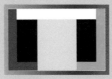

3 columns fixed centered

Dynamic with header & footer

TEMPLATE CULTURE
THE WEB

▼ TEMPLATE CULTURE

Technical standards, recognisability and reproducibility largely determine the visual character of information.

▼ TYPOGRAPHY

Every image that has become iconic through fame, repetition and familiarity is seen and used as typography.

TASTE IS CLASS-BASED

The new generation of designers are not so much looking for a way to develop their own visual language, but see designing as making a choice between the styles and trends that are offered by these software programs. They combine and manipulate existing styles and are often totally unaware of the fact that the image languages with which they work were once developed by designers. They lack knowledge and cannot make the reference to their predecessors.

▼ USER GENERATED STYLE

Images and products today are mostly generated and constructed automatically by the computer; styles and objects are calculated, rendered, and visualised with a single press of a button.

INVEST IN *BANKRUPTCY*

I **MY CRISIS**

ANOTHER DAY ANOTHER WAR

YES! **YOU CAN'T**

UNFRIEND YOUR LOVER

VIRAL *RESTRUCTURING*

CONSUME YOUR LOSSES

EMBRACE *STAGNATION*

SUPPORT
MY
CRISIS

T-shirt label:
MADE
FOR
ASIA

THE
INSTITUTION
IS THE
MESSAGE

ETHICS
IS MORAL PUNK

BECOME
PRINCESS

romantic
mobility
♥

BUY MORE
Consume Less

NETWORKING IS
A GREAT WAY TO
WASTE TIME
BEFORE DYING

NANO SHOOTS VIDEO

NANOTECHNOLOGY IS SOOOO... NEW.

NO ONE IS REALLY SURE WHAT WILL COME OF IT.

▼ HOW NANOTECHNOLOGY WORKS

There's an unprecedented multidisciplinary convergence of scientists dedicated to the study of a world so small, we can't see it - even with a light microscope. That world is the field of nanotechnology, the realm of atoms and nanostructures. Even so, predictions range from the ability to reproduce things like diamonds and food to the world being devoured by self-replicating nanorobots. A nanometer (nm) is one-billionth of a meter, smaller than the wavelength of visible light and a hundred-thousandth the width of a human hair [SOURCE: BERKELEY LAB].

SMALL SMALLER SMALLEST

▼ SERIOUS NANOTECHNOLOGY

Serious nanotechnology runs the gamut from things we can't do yet--so-called "spooky" nanotechnology like build-anything molecular assemblers and bacterium-size supercomputers--to things we are beginning to be able to do like diagnostic nanosensors and superstrong carbon nanotube materials. GLENN REYNOLDS, LAW PROFESSOR AT THE UNIVERSITY OF TENNESSEE

NANO

IS A LOVELY BRAND NAME.

THE BEST BRAND NAME IS A FOUR-LETTER WORD, SIMPLE, CRISP AND TO THE POINT.

How New is Nanotechnology?
In 1959, physicist and future Nobel prize winner Richard Feynman gave a lecture to the American Physical Society called "There's Plenty of Room at the Bottom." The focus of his speech was the field of miniaturisation and how he believed man would create increasingly smaller, powerful devices.

In 1986, K. Eric Drexler wrote *Engines of Creation* and introduced the term 'nanotechnology'. Scientific research has really expanded over the last decade. Inventors and corporations aren't far behind - today, more than 13,000 patents registered with the U.S. Patent Office have the word 'nano' in them [source: U.S. Patent and Trademark Office].

▼ THE FUTURE OF NANO

In the world of *Star Trek*, machines called replicators can produce practically any physical object, from weapons to a steaming cup of Earl Grey tea. Long considered to be exclusively the product of science fiction, today some people believe replicators are a very real possibility. They call it molecular manufacturing, and if it ever does become a reality, it could drastically change the world.

▼ GREEN?

Nano, it's not green, it's totalitarian from protestors.

MINI!

▼ CRITIC OF NANOTECHNOLOGY

Many nanotechnology experts feel that these applications are well outside the realm of possibility, at least for the foreseeable future. They caution that the more exotic applications are only theoretical. Some worry that nanotechnology will end up like virtual reality - in other words, the hype surrounding nanotechnology will continue to build until the limitations of the field become public knowledge, and then interest (and funding) will quickly dissipate. KEVIN BONSOR AND JONATHAN STRICKLAND

21ˢᵗ CENTURY
LANGUAGE

- ○ *RFID*
- ○ *NANO*
- ○ *WIFI*

OK

▼ WRITING IS WORK

We should be wary of claims made for the intrinsic virtue of online platforms by participants and commentators who want to believe in a new model of open-access criticism driven by the comment box. They suggest that these collective voices will somehow amount to a more democratic and reliable alternative because the aggregated "wisdom of the crowd" must necessarily surpass the partisan insights of an individual critic.[1] But opinion is not criticism and the number of people saying something is no guarantee of its power to illuminate. Writing will always require effort - both the writer's and the reader's. In whatever medium criticism happens to appear, the yardsticks to evaluate it remain the same: degree of timeliness, breadth of knowledge, originality of thought, depth of perception, and quality of argument and expression. RICK POYNOR

1 See, for instance, James Surowiecki, The Wisdom of Crowds: Why the Many Are Smarter Than the Few and How Collective Wisdom Shapes Business, Economies, Societies, and Nations (2004).

READ ME!

▼ ANALOGUE CULTURE

I once wrote novels with a manual typewriter. This may seem like bizarrely archaic behaviour, but once it was a thoroughly integrated, well rehearsed, well understood form of something-or-other. 'Analogue culture' we might call that now. BRUCE STERLING

BOOK TITLE MENU

ACCELERATE YOUR SELF-AFFIRMATION

BACK-END STRATEGIES

BUILDING CONTROL

COPY-PASTE THE PROCESS

CORPORATE HERITAGE

YOU ARE NOT A PRODUCT

IF LEONARDO WAS AN ARCHITECT

EVERYONE IS A CURATOR

EVERYONE IS A FRIEND

FASHIONISTAS ARE GETTING NERVOUS

FORM FOLLOWS FORMAT

FOLLOW MY DESIGN

FREE-RANGE IMAGERY

FROM ART DECO TO INFO DECO

HISTORY OF INNOVATION

I WANT TO COPY YOU

IN THE AGE OF OVERLOAD

LEARNING FROM LOUIS VUITTON

MARKET OF AESTHETICS

MASTER CONTENT

NETWORK WITH US

OFF THE SHELF NEWS

PREMIUM BABBLE

REAL-TIME FASHION

RESOURCES DESIGN THE WORLD

SPEAKERS ACADEMY

THE PROCESS IS THE PRODUCT

TEMPLATE CULTURE

VISIONARY IN RESIDENCE

WHAT ARE YOU CREATING?

BECOMING PRINCESS

MULTITASKING IS FOR THE POOR

UNFRIEND YOUR LOVER

DESIGN YOUR STRUGGLE

STOP READING START BROWSING

UP WITH EGO INFLATION

NETWORKING IS A GREAT WAY TO WASTE TIME BEFORE DYING

▼ HISTORY

For thousands of years, man would use only his body to communicate. And after a long period of text culture, the image and social media culture brings us via Internet back to those primaeval times of the tactile and oral man who experiences the world very directly and emotionally.

▼ CULTURAL PRODUCTION

Increasingly simple graphic software allows everyone to process images and make videos. Social networks and video platforms enable lightning-fast distribution. DIY is more satisfying than passive absorption. Young cultural consumers have become producers and sometimes do not realise their activities are part of a cultural field.

DO YOU KNOW WHAT IS NOT IMPORTANT?

▼ COPY-PASTE

Cultural forms are, as it were, freely appropriated, revised and redacted, meaning traditional notions like originality, authenticity and creation are gradually being replaced by copy/paste, sampling and montage.

Buy More!

CONSUME™
LESS

▼ PARTICIPATION

The success of YouTube and Wikipedia is down to the huge crowds of people presenting visual material, doing research and collaborating but also criticising, ranking, selecting and assigning meaning.

THE BOUNDARY BETWEEN CONSUMERS AND PRODUCERS IS DISAPPEARING

▼ SOCIAL SOFTWARE

Important are the tools for social communication and sharing of media, information, and knowledge such as web browsers, email clients, instant messaging clients, wikis, social bookmarking, social citation tools, virtual worlds, and so on. LEV MANOVICH

▼ MOVING IMAGE

The explosion of cultural production in the area of the moving image has become uncontrollable. Noteworthy videos and images float around the Web en masse. We sometimes don't even know who their makers are.

▼ SOCIAL SPACE

At the moment, Facebook and Twitter are the most popular forms of communication. These social community programs are extremely unattractive environments in which very many people nevertheless daily spend their time. This form of communication brings back memories of the early days of the Internet, when technique held considerable sway over aesthetics.

▼ DO IT YOURSELF

Do you feel lame after sitting alone with your camera, angling your jaw for a "spontaneous" face? Don't. We've all done the self-shot. With the metempsychosis of all social behaviour into Facebook, Twitter, and Whatever-the-shit-er, we're all well on the way to becoming our own avatars. GEERT LOVINK

▶ SOCIAL SOFTWARE

INFLATION OF SELF-PROMOTION

▼ DE-FRIENDING

Matthieu Laurette has de-friended more than 1400 "friends" and it's only the beginning...

Three Trends *in Web 2.0*

SOCIALITY IS THE CAPACITY OF BEING SEVERAL THINGS AT ONCE G. H. MEAD

Web 2.0 has three distinguishing features: it is easy to use; it facilitates the social element, such as linking to each other; and users can upload their own content in whatever form, be it pictures, videos or text. It is all about publishing and production. Here I will discuss three recent Internet trends: the colonisation of real-time, comment culture and the rise of extreme opinions, and the emergence of 'national webs'.

THE COLONISATION OF REAL-TIME

TREND 1

There is a fundamental shift away from the static archive towards the 'flow' and the 'river'. We see this occurring in metaphors like Google Wave. Twitter is the most visible symptom of this transitory tendency. Who responds to yesterday's references?

History is something you want to get rid of.

Silicon Valley is gearing up for the colonisation of real-time, away from the static web 'page' that still refers to the newspaper. Users don't feel the need anymore to store information and the 'cloud' facilitates this liberation movement. We'll save our files at Google or elsewhere, and can get rid of the clumsy all-purpose PCs.

AWAY WITH THE UGLY OFFICE FURNITURE!

The Web has turned into an ephemeral environment. Some have even said goodbye to the very idea of 'search' because it is a time-consuming activity with often unsatisfactory outcomes. This could potentially, be the point where the Google empire starts to crumble - and that is why they are keen to be at the forefront of what Paul Virilio already described ages ago.

Google Wave merges email instant messaging, wikis and social networking. It integrates the feeds of Facebook, Twitter, etc. accounts into one real live event happening on the screen. It is a meta online tool for real-time communication. Wave looks like you're sitting on the banks of a river, watching the flow go by. It is no longer the case that you approach the PC with a question and then dive into the archive. The Internet as a whole is going real-time, in an attempt to come closer to the messiness, the complexities of the actually existing social world. What is one step forward means two steps back in terms of design.

Just look at the clumsy design of Twitter, which reassembles ASCII email and SMS messages on your 2001 cell phone.

TO WHAT EXTENT IS THIS A CONSCIOUS VISUAL SPECIAL EFFECT?

Typo rawness html-style may not be a technical imperfection but rather points at the unfinishedness of the Eternal Now in which we are caught.

THERE IS NO SPACE FOR SLOW MEDIA

The pacemaker of the real-time Internet is 'microblogging' but we can also think of the social networking sites and their urge to pull real-time data out of its users: "What are you doing?" Give us your self-shot. "What's on your mind?" Expose your impulses. Frantically updated blogs are part of this inclination, as are frequently updated news sites. The driving technology behind this is the constant evolution of RSS feeds, which makes it possible to get instant updates of what's happening elsewhere on the Web. The increasing proliferation of mobile plays a significant role in the background as the main facilitator to 'mobilise' your computer, the social network, your video and photo camera, audio devices, and eventually also your TV out in the open. The miniaturisation of hardware combined with wireless connectivity makes it possible for technology to become an invisible part of everyday life. Web 2.0 applications are responses to this trend and attempt to subtract value out of every situation we find ourselves in.

THE MACHINE CONSTANTLY WANTS TO KNOW WHAT WE THINK, WHAT CHOICES WE MAKE, WHERE WE GO, AND WHO WE TALK TO.

THERE IS NO EVIDENCE THAT THE WORLD IS BECOMING MORE VIRTUAL.

The cyber prophets were wrong here. The virtual wants to penetrate and map out our real lives and social relationships.

THE VIRTUAL IS BECOMING MORE REAL.

All the investment is there, and moving away from Second Life, virtualisation, and pretending to be someone else.

WE ARE NO LONGER ENCOURAGED TO PRETEND TO BE SOMEONE ELSE, BUT TO BE OURSELVES.

WE CONSTANTLY LOG IN, CREATE PROFILES IN ORDER TO PRESENT OUR- SELVES ON THE GLOBAL MARKETPLACE OF JOBS, FRIENDSHIPS AND LOVE.

We can have multiple passions but only one ID. Trust is the oil of global capitalism and the security state. The earlier idea that the virtual was there to liberate you from your old self has broken down. It is all about self-management and techno-sculpturing: how do you shape the Self in real-time flow? In that sense there is no time for design. There is no time for doubt. System response cannot deal with ambivalence.

NETIZENS AND THE RISE OF EXTREME OPINIONS

TREND 2

Where has the rational and balanced 'netizen' gone, the well-behaved online citizen? The Internet seems to have become an echo chamber for extreme opinions. Is Web 2.0 getting out of control? At first glance, the idea of the netizen is a mid-1990s response to the first wave of users that took over the Net. The netizen moderates, cools down heated debates and first of all responds in a non-repressive manner. The netizen does not represent the Law, is no authority, and acts like a personal advisor, a guide in a new universe. The netizen role is proposed in the spirit of good conduct and corporate citizenship. Users had to take social responsibility themselves. It was not a call for government regulation - and was explicitly designed to keep legislators out of the Net. Until 1990, the late academic stage of the Net, it was presumed that all users knew the rules (also called netiquette), and would behave accordingly. Of course this wasn't always the case (in the end, we're all too human), so, when misbehaviour was noticed the individual would be convinced to stop spamming, bullying, etc. This was no longer possible after 1995 when the Internet opened up to the general public and the

World Wide Web with its browsers that made it so much easier to use. Because of the rapid growth, the code of conduct, developed over time by IT engineers and scientists, could no longer be passed on from one user to the next.

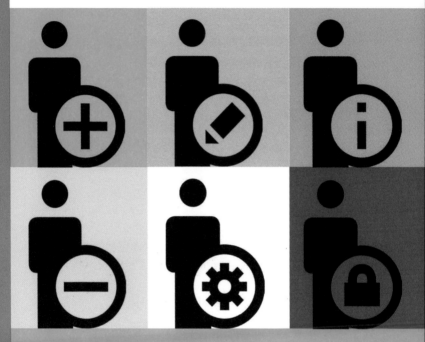

At the time, the Net was seen as a global medium that could not easily be controlled by national legislation. Perhaps there was some truth in this. Cyberspace was out of control, but in a nice and still innocent way. It was cute and somewhat desperate that in a room next to the prime minister of Bavaria in Munich, authorities would install a task force to police the Bavarian part of the Internet. At the time we had a good laugh about such a hopeless gesture.

After 9/11 and the dotcom crash things changed dramatically. A good decade later there are tons of legislation, government bodies and a whole arsenal of software tools to oversee the National Web, as it is now called. Retrospectively, it is quite easy to deconstruct the rational 'netizen' approach as a libertarian 'Gestalt', a figure from the neo-liberal age of deregulation, but the issues have only grown exponentially, and not gone away. These days we would probably frame it more as a part of education programmes in schools and general awareness campaigns.

Identity theft is a serious business.

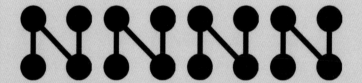

Cyberbullying amongst young kids does happen and both parents and teachers need to know how to identify and respond to it. Much like in the mid-1990s, we're still faced with the problem of 'massification'. The sheer user numbers and intensity in with which people engage with the Internet is phenomenal. What perhaps has changed is that many no longer believe that the Internet community can sort out these issues itself. The internet has penetrated society to such an extent that they have become one and the same.

In times of global recession, rising nationalism, ethnic tensions and collective obsession with the Islam Question, comment cultures inside Web 2.0 seem to be a major concern for media regulators and the police. Blogs, forums and social networking sites invite users to leave behind short messages.

It is in particular the young people who react impulsively to events, often posting death threats to politicians and celebrities without realising what they just did. The professional monitoring of comments is becoming a serious business. Just to give two Dutch examples: Marokko.nl has to oversee 50.000 postings on a daily basis, and right-wing Telegraaf news site gets 15.000 comments on its selected news items daily. Populist blogs like Geen Stijl encourage users to post extreme judgments - a proven tactic to draw attention to the site. Whereas some sites have internal policies to delete racist remarks, death threats and liable content, others encourage their users to do post exactly that, all in the name of freedom of speech. Current software enables users to leave behind short statements, often without the possibility for others to respond.

Web 2.0 wasn't designed to facilitate debate.

The 'terror of informality' inside 'walled gardens' like Facebook is now increasingly becoming a problem. If the Web goes real-time, there is less time for reflection, and more technology that facilitates impulsive blather. This development will only further invite authorities to interfere in online mass conversations. Will interface design bring a solution here? Bots are increasingly playing a role in the automated policing of large websites. But bots merely work in the background, and do their silent jobs for the powers that be. How can users regain control and navigate complex threads? Should they unleash their own bots and design tools in order to reconquer 'personal information autonomy', as David d'Heilly once coined it?

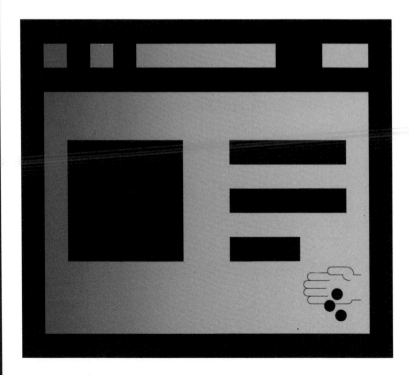

THE RISE OF THE NATIONAL WEBS

TREND 3

Due to rise of the worldwide internet user base, the focus has shifted from the global potential towards local, regional and national exchanges. Only around 25% of the content is in English these days. Most conversations are no longer happening in English.

A host of new technologies is geo-sensitive.

What people care about first and foremost is what happens in their immediate surroundings - and there is nothing wrong with that. This was predicted in the nineties, it just took a while to be implemented. Background of the 'national web' is the development of increasingly sophisticated tools to oversee the national IP range (the IP addresses allocated to a country). These technologies can be used in two directions: to block users from outside the country, to see the national television programs online and visit public libraries such as in Norway and Australia (in the case of new ABC online services), and to prevent citizens from visiting overseas sites (Mainland Chinese not being able to visit You Tube, Facebook, etc.).

The 'democratization' of the internet really only happened over the past 5-10 years and the Obama campaign was a significant landmark in this process. Representation and participation, in this context, are outworn concepts. It presumes that firms and politicians have a goal and then invite others to contribute. In this age of large corporations, big NGOs and government departments, it is all too easy to deploy Web 2.0 strategies as a part of your overall communication plan. This open-knowledge-for-all has not arrived everywhere yet, true – and there is still a role to play for the Web 2.0 consultant. But Web 2.0 is certainly no longer a 'Geheimtip'. There is already a lot known about web demographics, usability requirements, and what application to use in which context. One would, for instance, not use MySpace to approach senior citizen. It is also known that young people are reluctant to use Twitter. It's just not their thing. These are all top-down considerations.

IT GETS MORE INTERESTING IF YOU ASK THE NETIZEN 2.0 QUESTION.

How will people themselves start to utilize these tools bottom-up? Will activists start to use their own Web 2.0 tools?

Remember that social networking sites did not originate in a social movement setting. They were developed as post-dotcom responses to the silly e-commerce wave of the late 1990s that had no concept of what users were looking for online. Instead of regarding users merely as consumers of goods and services, inside Web 2.0 people are pressed to produce as much data as possible. From the so-called 'user generated content', profiles are abstracted, which are then sold to advertisers as direct marketing customer data. Users do not experience the parasitic nature of Web 2.0 immediately.

From a political point of view, the rise of national webs is an ambivalent development.

In design terms it's all about localisation, of fonts, brands and contexts.

Whereas communicating in one's own language, not having to use Latin script keyboards and domain names, can be seen as a liberating necessity to bring on board the remaining 80% of the world population that is not yet using the Internet, the new digital enclosures also present a direct threat to the free and open exchanges the Internet once facilitated. The Internet turns out to be neither the problem nor the solution for the global recession. As an indifferent bystander it doesn't lend itself easily as a revolutionary tool. It's part of the Green New Deal - but it is not driving these reforms. Increasingly, authoritarian regimes such as Iran are making tactical use of the Web in order to crack down on the opposition. Against all predictions, the Great Chinese Firewall is remarkably successful in keeping out hostile content, whilst monitoring the internal population on an unprecedented scale.

The Internet turns out to be neither the problem nor the solution for the global recession.

Contributors:

Matthew Fuller is David Gee Reader in Digital Media at the Centre for Cultural Studies, Goldsmiths College, University of London. He is the author of *Media Ecologies: Materialist Energies in Art and Technoculture* (MIT Press, 2005). www.gold.ac.uk

Alexander R. Galloway is the author of *Gaming: Essays on Algorithmic Culture* and associate professor in the Department of Culture and Communication at New York University. He has a PhD in Literature from Duke University. www.alexgalloway.net

Mieke Gerritzen is director of the Graphic Design Museum in the Netherlands. Gerritzen is an award-winning designer and organises events, presentations, exhibitions and conferences worldwide. www.all-media.eu and www.graphicdesignmuseum.com

Sophie Krier explores the peripheries of the design field, with a focus on film, writing and temporary social interventions. She is currently developing scenarios for public space and editing a new design journal entitled *Field Essays*. www.sophiekrier.com

Geert Lovink is an Internet critic and director of the Institute of Network Cultures. Lovink publishes books, signals and criticises trends of Internet culture and organises international conferences. www.networkcultures.org

Peter Lunenfeld is a critic and theorist of digital media. He is a professor in the Design Media Arts department at UCLA, director of the Institute for Technology and Aesthetics (ITA), and founder of the Mediawork Pamphlet series. www.peterlunenfeld.com

Ellen Lupton is Curator of Contemporary Design at the Cooper-Hewitt and Director of the Graphic Design MFA Program at Maryland Institute College of Art, Baltimore. She is author of several books including *Design Culture Now* and *D.I.Y.: Design It Yourself.* www.designwritingresearch.org

Lev Manovich is a Professor in the Visual Arts Department, University of California San Diego, and Director of the Software Studies Initiative. Lev Manovich's books include *Software Takes Command, Soft Cinema* and *The Language of New Media.* www.manovich.net

Koert van Mensvoort is an artist/scientist. He holds a PhD in industrial design from Eindhoven University of Technology. His most profound experience in life, so far, has been the discovery of Next Nature; nature changes along with us. www.nextnature.net

Metahaven is a studio for design and research based in Amsterdam and Brussels. Metahaven works in visual identity and architecture, both with clients and independently. www.metahaven.net

Henk Oosterling is a senior lecturer in the Faculty of Philosophy at Erasmus University Rotterdam. He lectures on dialectic methods, French philosophy and differential thinking, intercultural philosophy and aesthetics. www.oosterling.nl

Merijn Oudenampsen is a political and urban researcher. Besides working on issues such as city branding, the creative city, and urban redevelopment more broadly, he is currently concerned with the spectacular ascendance of Dutch populist politics. www.flexmens.org

Rick Poynor is a British writer on design, graphic design, typography and visual culture. He began as a general visual arts journalist, working on *Blueprint* magazine in London. After founding *Eye* magazine, he has focused increasingly on visual communication.

Ned Rossiter is Associate Professor of Network Cultures at the University of Nottingham in Ningbo, China, and Adjunct Senior Research Fellow at the Centre for Cultural Research at the University of Western Sydney, Australia. www.nedrossiter.org

Stefan Sagmeister is a New York-based graphic designer and typographer. He has his own design firm - Sagmeister Inc. - in New York City. He has designed album covers for Lou Reed, The Rolling Stones, David Byrne and Pat Metheny. www.sagmeister.com

Clay Shirky is an American writer, consultant and teacher on the social and economic effects of Internet technologies. He is the author of several books including *Here Comes Everybody: The Power of Organizing Without Organizations* (2008) www.shirky.com

Bruce Sterling is one of the main voices of the cyberpunk movement. In the 1980s, he promoted a worldview and aesthetic that strongly influenced the generation that came of age with the computer revolution. www.wired.com/beyond_the_beyond/

McKenzie Wark is the author of *A Hacker Manifesto* (Harvard 2004), *Gamer Theory* (Harvard 2007) and various other things. He is associate dean of Eugene Lang College, The New School, New York. www.newschool.edu

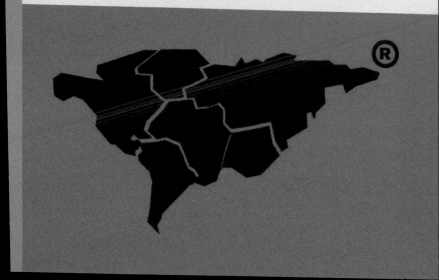

Textual quotes by:

Christopher Steiner	www.forbes.com
Mariëtte Dölle	www.tentrotterdam.nl/
Charles Leadbeater	www.charlesleadbeater.net
Andrew Keen	www.andrewkeen.typepad.com/
Imperva.com	www.imperva.com/
Michael Stevenson	www.whateverbutton.com
David Nieborg	www.gamespace.nl
Dave Winer	www.davenet.scripting.com/
Frank Kalshoven, Martijn Bennis	www.denieuwereporter.nl/
Bas Broekhuizen	www.denieuwereporter.nl/
Jaron Lanier	www.well.com/~jaron/
Willem Koch	www.tnt.nl
Jodi Dean	www.jdeanicite.typepad.com/
Jacob Nielsen	www.useit.com/
Jeff Jarvis	www.buzzmachine.com/
MoOM	www.coudal.com/moom/
Berkeley Lab	www.lbl.gov/
Glenn Reynolds	www.glennreynolds.com/
Kevin Bonsor, Jonathan Strickland	www.science.howstuffworks.com

Visual quotes by:

Jack van Wijk	www.win.tue.nl/~vanwijk/
IKEA	www.ikea.com
Klaus Staeck	www.staeck.de
Shepard Fairley	www.obeygiant.com
Andy Warhol	www.warholfoundation.org/
Leonardo Da Vinci	www.en.wikipedia.org/wiki/Leonardo
Universal Icons - page 124-139	www.blog.picol.org/pre-release-picol-icons/
Drawings - page 064-081	www.freepatentsonline.com/
Gerd Arntz	www.gerdarntz.org/
CSS Templates and Samples	www.alistapart.com
Heidegger	www.st-andrews.ac.uk
Computer worker	www.nobodyhere.com

Concept and Design	Mieke Gerritzen
Editors	Geert Lovink and Mieke Gerritzen
Production	All Media Foundation, Amsterdam
Publisher	BIS Publishers, Amsterdam
Translation	Laura Martz
Unbylined texts by	Mieke Gerritzen

First Edition 2010
ISBN: 978-90-6369-227-8

All Media Foundation
Rustenburgerstraat 4
1074 ET Amsterdam
The Netherlands
info@all-media.info
www.all-media.eu

BIS Publishers
Het Sieraad
Postjesweg 1
1057 DT Amsterdam
The Netherlands
T +31 (0)20 5150230
F +31 (0)20 5150239
bis@bispublishers.nl
www.bispublishers.nl

Printed in China

Thanks to:
Graphic Design Museum
www.graphicdesignmuseum.com
Institute for Network Cultures
www.networkcultures.org

B
GRAPHIC
DESIGN
MUSEUM